SPIRIT OF PLACE
⬩ VENICE ⬩

She is the Shakespeare of cities – unchallenged,
incomparable, and beyond envy.

JOHN ADDINGTON SYMONDS, *SKETCHES AND STUDIES IN ITALY*, 1879

Arcade Publishing
New York

IMPRESSIONS OF VENICE

Nothing in the world that you have ever heard of Venice is equal to the magnificent and stupendous reality. The wildest visions of the Arabian Nights are nothing to the piazza of St Mark, and the first impression of the inside of the church. The gorgeous and wonderful reality of Venice is beyond the fancy of the wildest dreamer. Opium couldn't build such a place, and enchantment couldn't shadow it forth in a vision... It has never been rated high enough. It is a thing you would shed tears to see.

CHARLES DICKENS, LETTER, 1844

Venice is like eating an entire box of chocolate liqueurs at one go.

TRUMAN CAPOTE, QUOTED IN *THE OBSERVER*, 26 NOVEMBER 1961

REALIZING A DREAM

To taste in all their fullness his first impressions of Venice, the traveller should arrive there by sea, at mid-day, when the sun is high. . . He who comes for the first time to Venice by this route realizes a dream – his only dream perhaps ever destined to be surpassed by the reality; and if he knows how to enjoy the things of Nature, if he can take delight in silver-grey and rose-coloured reflections in water, if he loves light and colour, the picturesque life of Italian squares and streets, the good humour of the people and their gentle speech, which seems like the twittering of birds, let him only allow himself to live for a little time under the sky of Venice, and he has before him a season of happiness without alloy.

CHARLES YRIATE, *VENICE*, 1880

VENICE AS A THEATRE

I don't know why it happened that on this occasion I was more than ever struck with that queer air of sociability, of cousinship and family life, which makes up half the expression of Venice. Without streets and vehicles, the uproar of wheels, the brutality of horses, and with its little winding ways where people crowd together, where voices sound as in the corridors of a house, where the human step circulates as if it skirted the angles of furniture and shoes never wear out, the place has the character of an immense collective apartment, in which Piazza San Marco is the most ornamented corner, and palaces and churches, for the rest, play the part of great divans of repose, tables of entertainment, expanses of decoration. And somehow the splendid common domicile, familiar, domestic and resonant, also resembles a theatre with its actors clicking over bridges and, in straggling processions, tripping along fondamentas. As you sit in your gondola the footways that in certain parts edge the canals assume to the eye the importance of a stage, meeting it at the same angle, and the Venetian figures, moving to and fro against the battered scenery of their little houses of comedy, strike you as members of an endless dramatic troupe.

HENRY JAMES, *THE ASPERN PAPERS*, 1888

THE HORSES OF ST MARK

Before St Mark still glow his steeds of brass,
Their gilded collars glittering in the sun;
But is not Doria's menace come to pass?
Are they not *bridled*? – Venice, lost and won,
Her thirteen hundred years of freedom done,
Sinks like a seaweed into whence she rose!
Better be whelm'd beneath the waves, and shun,
Even in destruction's depth, her foreign foes,
From whom submission wrings an infamous repose.

LORD BYRON, *CHILDE HAROLD'S PILGRIMAGE*, 1816

THE PIAZZETTA AND DOGE'S PALACE

We were in our gondola by nine o'clock the next morning, and of course the first point we sought was the Piazza di San Marco. I am glad to find Ruskin calling the Palace of the Doges one of the two most perfect buildings in the world . . . This spot is a focus of architectural wonders: but the palace is the crown of them all. The double tier of columns and arches, with the rich sombreness of their finely outlined shadows, contrasts satisfactorily with the warmth and light and more continuous surface of the upper part. Even landing on the Piazzetta, one has a sense, not only of being in an entirely novel scene, but one where the ideas of a foreign race have poured themselves in without yet mingling indistinguishably with the pre-existent Italian life. But this is felt yet more strongly when one has passed along the Piazzetta and arrived in front of San Marco, with its low arches and domes and minarets. But perhaps the most striking point to take one's stand on is just in front of the white marble guard-house flanking the great tower – the guard-house with Sansovino's iron gates before it. On the left is San Marco, with the two square pillars from St Jean d'Acre, standing as isolated trophies; on the right the Piazzetta extends between the Doge's palace and the Palazzo Reale to the tall columns from Constantinople; and in front of the elaborate gateway leading to the white marble Scala di Giganti, in the courtyard of the Doge's palace.

GEORGE ELIOT, FROM JOHN WALTER CROSS, *GEORGE ELIOT'S LIFE*, 1885

RUSKIN IN ST MARK'S

As we advance slowly, the vast tower of St Mark seems to lift itself visibly forth from the level field of chequered stones; and, on each side, the countless arches prolong themselves into ranged symmetry, as if the rugged and irregular houses that pressed together above us in the dark alley had been struck back into sudden obedience and lovely order, and all their rude casements and broken walls had been transformed into arches charged with goodly sculpture, and fluted shafts of delicate stone.

And well may they fall back, for beyond those troops of ordered arches there rises a vision out of the earth, and all the great square seems to have opened from it in a kind of awe, that we may see it far away;—a multitude of pillars and white domes, clustered into a long low pyramid of coloured light; a treasure-heap, it seems, partly of gold, and partly of opal, and mother-of-pearl, hollowed beneath into five great vaulted porches, ceiled with fair mosaic, and beset with sculpture of alabaster, clear as amber and delicate as ivory,—sculpture fantastic and involved, of palm leaves and lilies, and grapes and pomegranates, and birds clinging and fluttering among the branches, all twined together into an endless network of buds and plumes.

JOHN RUSKIN, *THE STONES OF VENICE*, 1851-53

THE INTERIOR OF ST MARK'S

I thought I entered a Cathedral, and went in and out among its many arches: traversing its whole extent. A grand and dreamy structure, of immense proportions; golden with old mosaics; redolent of perfumes; dim with the smoke of incense; costly in treasure of precious stones and metals, glittering through iron bars; holy with the bodies of deceased saints; rainbow-hued with windows of stained glass; dark with carved woods and coloured marbles; obscure in its vast heights and lengthened distances, shining with silver lamps and winking lights; unreal, fantastic, solemn, inconceivable throughout.

CHARLES DICKENS, *PICTURES FROM ITALY*, 1846

'WHITE SWAN OF CITIES . . .'

White swan of cities, slumbering in thy nest
   So wonderfully built among the reeds
   Of the lagoon, that fences thee and feeds,
   As sayest thy old historian and thy guest!
White water-lily, cradled and caressed
   By ocean streams, and from the silt and weeds
   Lifting thy golden filaments and seeds,
Thy sun-illumined spires, thy crown and crest!
White phantom city, whose untrodden streets
   Are rivers, and whose pavements are the shifting
   Shadows of the palaces and strips of sky;
I wait to see thee vanish like the fleets
   Seen in mirage, or towers of cloud uplifting
   In air their unsubstantial masonry.

HENRY WADSWORTH LONGFELLOW, VENICE, 1876

VENETIAN PALACES

 What shall I tell you of the famous palaces? They are more laboured externally, and have less simplicity and grandeur than I had expected to see; but many of them are magnificent houses. All stand on a canal, very many on the principal one; but they all extend far back towards the streets, and can be entered as well by land as by water. There is a large hall or vestibule below, into which one first enters on quitting the gondola; and it is very usual to see one or more gondolas in it, as one sees carriages in a court. The rooms above are often as rich as those of royal residences, and many capital pictures are still found in them. The floors are, almost invariably, of the composition which I have already mentioned as resembling variegated marble. A much smaller proportion of them than of those at Rome appear to be regularly occupied by their owners.

JAMES FENIMORE COOPER, *EXCURSIONS IN ITALY*, 1838

ON THE RIALTO

The traveller who delights to linger on St Mark's Place, in the Basilica, at the Ducal Palace, in the museums and churches, should also halt long and often at the Rialto. This is a corner with a character quite its own; here crowd together, laden with fruit and vegetables, the black boats that come from the islands to provision Venice, the great hulls laden with *cocomeri*, *angurie*, with gourds and water-melons piled in mountains of colour; there the gondolas jostle, and the gondoliers chatter like birds in their Venetian idiom; there, too, are the fishermen in their busy, noisy, black-looking market, an assemblage of strange craft and strange types of humanity; and as a pleasant contrast, on the steps of the bridge and stepping before the jewellers' shops, are girls from the different quarters of Venice, from Cannaregio, Dorso Duro, San Marco, and Sante Croce, and from every corner of the town, come to buy the coloured handkerchiefs they deck themselves in, and jewellery of delicately worked gold, or bright glass beads from Murano, or glass balls iridescent with green, blue and pink; while, wrapped in old grey shawls and showing only their wrinkled profiles and silver locks, the old women of the Rialto drag their slippers up the steps, and glide among the crowd hiding under the folds of their aprons the strange fries they have just bought from those keepers of open-air provision stalls who ply their trade on the approaches to the Rialto.

CHARLES YRIATE, *VENICE*, 1880

A RAINY DAY IN VENICE

The charm of Venice grows on me strangely; at first I had no real personal impression: and then one rainy day, when the wind, with the sound of bells in it, blew up the Grand Canal, and everything was half blotted in a veil of rain, I suddenly felt all the melancholy charm – the charm of silence and beauty and decay. The strangest thing is to go at night, as we often do in our little boat, up the Grand Canal, & then turn in anywhere, and lose ourselves in the blackness and silence. The great palaces are so high that these little canals seem almost like subterranean rivers, save for the strip of sky and the vague stars above. Sometimes we come suddenly, round a corner, on a square with yellow lights & footsteps & music. Then we glide away into the darkness till at last we come out by the Grand Canal again.

LOGAN PEARSALL SMITH, LETTER, 15 NOVEMBER 1895

Prendergast

Maurice B. Prendergast

COSMOPOLITAN VENICE

When the Venetians stroll out in the evening, they do not avoid the Piazza San Marco, where the tourists are, as the Romans do with Doney's on the Via Veneto. The Venetians go to look at the tourists, and the tourists look back at them. It is all for the ear and eye, this city, but primarily for the eye. Built on water, it is an endless succession of reflections and echoes a mirroring. Contrary to popular belief, there are no back canals where the tourist will not meet himself, with a camera, in the person of the other tourist crossing the little bridge. And no word can be spoken in the city that is not an echo of something said before. '*Mais, c'est aussi cher que Paris!*' exclaims a Frenchman in a restaurant, unaware that he repeats Montaigne. The complaint against foreigners, voiced by a foreigner, chimes querulously through the ages, in unison with the medieval monk who found St Mark's Square filled with 'Turks, Libyans, Parthians, and other monsters of the sea'. Today it is the Germans we complain of, and no doubt they complain of the Americans, in the same words.

MARY MCCARTHY, *VENICE OBSERVED*, 1961

VENETIAN BACKWATERS

After dinner, I went out alone, into the heart of the enchanted city where I found myself in the middle of strange purlieus like a character in the *Arabian Nights*. It was very seldom that, in the course of my wanderings, I did not come across some strange and spacious *piazza* of which no guide-book, no tourist had ever told me. I had plunged into a network of little alleys, or *calli*, packed tightly together and dissecting in all directions with their furrows a chunk of Venice carved out between a canal and a lagoon, as if it had crystallised in accordance with these innumerable, tenuous and minute patterns. Suddenly, at the end of one of these alleys, it seemed as though a distension had occurred in the crystallised matter. A vast and splendid *campo* of which, in this network of little streets, I should never have guessed the scale, or even found room for it, spread out before me surrounded by charming palaces silvery in the moonlight. It was one of those architectural ensembles towards which, in any other town, the streets converge, lead you and point the way. Here it seemed to be deliberately concealed in a labyrinth of alleys, like those palaces in oriental tales whither mysterious agents convey by night a person who, brought back home before daybreak, can never find his way back to the magic dwelling which he ends by believing that he visited only in a dream.

MARCEL PROUST, *REMEMBRANCE OF THINGS PAST*, 1925

THE BRIDGE OF SIGHS

I stood in Venice, on the Bridge of Sighs;
A palace and a prison on each hand:
I saw from out the wave her structures rise
As from the stroke of the enchanter's wand:
A thousand years their cloudy wings expand
Around me, and a dying Glory smiles
O'er the far times, when many a subject land
Look'd to the winged Lion's marble piles,
Where Venice sate in state, throned on her hundred isles!

LORD BYRON, *CHILDE HAROLD'S PILGRIMAGE*, 1816

MEMORIES OF VENICE

Venice inspires at first an almost Corybantic rapture. From our earliest visits, if these have been measured by days rather than weeks, we carry away with us the memory of sunsets emblazoned in gold and crimson upon cloud and water; of violet domes and bell-towers etched against the orange of a western sky; of moonlight silvering breeze-rippled breadths of liquid blue; of distant islands shimmering in sun-litten haze; of music and black gliding boats; of labyrinthine darkness made for mysteries of love and crime; of statue-fretted palace fronts; of brazen clangour and a moving crowd, of pictures by earth's proudest painters, cased in gold on walls of council chambers where Venice sat enthroned a queen, where nobles swept the floor with robes of Tyrian brocade. These reminiscences will be attended by an ever-present sense of loneliness and silence in the world around; the sadness of a limitless horizon, the solemnity of an unbroken arch of heaven, the calm and greyness of evening on the lagoons, the pathos of a marble city crumbling to its grave in mud and brine.

JOHN ADDINGTON SYMONDS, *SKETCHES AND STUDIES IN ITALY*, 1879

Hilsen fra Venezia til Hvidøre.   P. Mønsted. 1928.

In a Gondola

I felt the spell at once, of this unique city,– this one and only Venice in all the world. Everywhere were gondolas,– gondolas moored at the quay, waiting for passengers; gondolas drawn up in front of palaces, waiting for their freight of dark-eyed Venetian girls; gondolas threading the mazes of the little canals, or sweeping down the Grand Canal, and drawing near each other now and then for a chat between the occupants.

All these gondolas are painted black. This is in accordance with an ancient law of the Republic, passed once upon a time when the decorations of the fascinating water-carriages were becoming too sumptuous for Republican morals. But even now many of the gondolas are very elegant. They are long and slender in shape, with a high beak pointed with steel; they are often superb in carving. Inside the little house in which you sit are soft cushions, and gilt-framed mirrors in which the piquant, dark-eyed faces of the Italian girls behold themselves in fascinating reflection.

ELLEN LOUISE CHANDLER MOULTON, *RANDOM RAMBLES*, 1881

The gondolas themselves are things of a most romantic and picturesque appearance; I can only compare them to moths of which a coffin might have been the chrysalis.

PERCY BYSSHE SHELLEY, LETTER TO THOMAS LOVE PEACOCK, 8 OCTOBER 1818

THE SKILL OF THE GONDOLIER

The Venetian gondola is as free and as graceful, in its gliding movement, as a serpent. . . The stern of the boat is decked over, and the gondolier stands there. He uses a single oar – a long blade, of course, for he stands nearly erect. A wooden peg, a foot and a half high, with two slight crooks or curves in one side of it and one in the other, projects above the starboard gunwhale. Against that peg the gondolier takes purchase with his oar, changing it at intervals to the other side of the peg or dropping it into another of the crooks, as the steering of the craft may demand – and how in the world he can back and fill, shoot straight ahead, or flirt suddenly round a corner, and make the oar stay in those insignificant notches, is a problem to me and a never diminishing matter of interest. I am afraid I study the gondolier's marvellous skill more than I do the sculptured palaces we glide among. He cuts a corner so closely, now and then, or misses another gondola by such an imperceptible hair-breadth that I feel myself 'scrooching', as the children say, just as one does when a buggy wheel grazes his elbow. But he makes all his calculations with the nicest precision, and goes darting in and out among a Broadway confusion of busy craft with the easy confidence of the educated hacksman. He never makes a mistake.

MARK TWAIN, *THE INNOCENTS ABROAD*, 1869

REGATTA ON THE GRAND CANAL

You seem to mention the regatta in a manner as if you would be pleased with a description of it. It is a race of boats: they are accompanied by vessels which they call Piotes, and Bichones, that are built at the expense of nobles and strangers that have a mind to display their magnificence; they are a sort of machine adorned with all that sculpture and gilding can do to make a shining appearance. Several of them cost one thousand pounds sterling, and I believe none less than five hundred; they are rowed by gondoliers dressed in rich habits, suitable to what they represent. There was enough of them to look like a little fleet, and I own I never saw a finer sight. It would be too long to describe every one in particular; I shall only name the principal:— the Signora Pisani Mocengio's represented the Chariot of the Night, drawn by four sea-horses, and showing the rising of the moon, accompanied with stars, the statues on each side representing the hours to the number of twenty-four, rowed by gondoliers in rich liveries, which were changed three times all of equal richness, and the decorations changed also to the dawn of Aurora and the midday sun, the statues being new dressed every time, the first in green, the second time in red, and the last blue, all equally laced with silver.

LADY MARY WORTLEY MONTAGU, LETTER, 1 JUNE 1740

I stirrd not from Padoa til Shrovetide, when all the world repaire to Venice to see the folly & madnesse of the Carnevall; the women, men & persons of all conditions disguising themselves in antique dresses, with extravagant Musique & a thousand gambols, & traversing the streetes from house to house, all places being then accessible & free to enter: There is abroad nothing but flinging of Eggs fill'd with sweete Waters & sometimes not over sweete; they also have a barbarous costome of hunting bulls about the Streetes & Piazzas, which is very dangerous, the passages being so narrow in that City. Likewise do the youth of the severall Wards & parrishes contend in other Masteries or pastimes, so that tis altogether impossible to recount the universal madnesse of this place during this time of licence. Now are the greate banks set up for those who will play at bassett, the Comedians have also liberty, & the Operas to Exercise. Witty pasquils are likewise thrown about, & the Mountebanks have their stages at every Corner.

JOHN EVELYN, *DIARY*, FEBRUARY 1646

I t was Shrove Tuesday in Venice, Carnival time. The sun had been shining on the city and on the lagoons all day long. It was one of those Shrove Tuesdays which recall the familiar proverb –

> 'Sunshine at Carnival,
> Fireside at Easter.'

But who cares about the chance of cold and gloom six weeks hence when to-day is fair and balmy? A hum of joyous, foolish voices echoed from those palace façades, and floated out seaward, and rang along the narrow *callé*, and drifted on the winding waterways, and resounded under the innumerable bridges; for everywhere in the City by the Sea, men, women, and children were making merry, and had given themselves up to a wild and childish rapture of unreasoning mirth, ready to explode into loud laughter at the sorriest jokes. An old man tapped upon the shoulder by a swinging paper lantern – a boy whose hat had been knocked off – a woman calling to her husband or her lover across the gay flotilla – anything was food for mirth on this holiday evening, while the great gold orb sank in the silvery lagoon, and all the sky over yonder Chioggia was dyed with the crimson afterglow, and the Chioggian fishing-boats were moving westward in all the splendour of their painted sails.

MARY ELIZABETH BRADDON, *THE VENETIANS*, 1892

REFLECTIONS IN VENICE

As the gondola brought us back along the Grand Canal, we watched the double line of palaces between which we passed reflect the light and angle of the sun upon their pink planks, and alter with them, seeming not so much private habitations and historic buildings as a chain of marble cliffs at the foot of which one goes out in the evening in a boat to watch the sunset. Seen thus, the buildings arranged along either bank of the canal made one think of objects of nature, but of a nature which seemed to have created its works with a human imagination.

MARCEL PROUST, *REMEMBRANCE OF THINGS PAST*, 1925

Decay in Venice

The sun shone upon Venice: all the bells were ringing. I stepped down into the black gondola, and sailed up into the dead street, where everything was water, not a foot-breadth upon which to walk. Large buildings stood with open doors, and with steps down to the water; the water ran into the great doorways, like a canal; and the palace-court itself seemed only a four-cornered well, into which people could sail, but scarcely turn the gondola. The water had left its greenish slime upon the walls: the great marble palaces seemed as if sinking together: in the broad windows, rough boards were nailed up to the gilded, half-decayed beams. The proud giant-body seemed to be falling away piecemeal; the whole had an air of depression about it. The ringing of the bells ceased, not a sound, excepting the splash of the oars in the water, was to be heard, and I still saw not a human being. The magnificent Venice lay like a dead swan upon the waves.

HANS ANDERSEN, *THE IMPROVISATORE*, 1845

SUNSHINE AND COLOUR

Two little red-shawled children are sitting on a seat opposite to me, counting their treasures; groups of small people, carrying just slightly smaller babies, are resting against the entrance to the gardens. I hear at every moment the slip-slop of heelless shoes dragging their way along the pavement, and catch the glimpse of the heels of brilliant stockings, red, stripes, white, occasionally a fine, ecclesiastical purple; now a whole flock of greenish yellow shawls passes, then, by itself, a bright green shawl, a grey, a blue, an amber; and scarcely two of all these coloured things are alike; the street flickers with colour, in the hot sunshine. Italian women are never at rest in their shawls, they are always unwinding them, resettling their folds, shifting them from head to shoulders, and back again, slipping out a ringed hand to sketch a whole series of gestures. And they are never in a hurry. They come and go, stop, form into groups, talk leisurely, and then go on their way, almost, I like to think, with the mechanical movement of a herd of cows, with the same deep sense of repose, of animal contentment, which comes of living in the sun.

ARTHUR SYMONS, *CITIES*, 1903

THE APPROACH OF WINTER

It is now late in October. The days are short but luminous still when the mists do not drift in from the lagoons of the Lido, or from the marshes of the low-lying lands beyond Mestre and Fucina. Boats still come in with rosy sunrise reflection shed on their orange sails, and take their loads of autumn apples and pears and walnuts to the fruit market above Rialto. But soon, very soon, it will be winter, and the gondolas will glide by with closed felze, and the water will be a troubled waste between the city and the Lido, and men will hurry with muffled heads over the square of Saint Mark when the Alpine wind blows, and the strange big ships creep on their piloted course tediously and timidly through the snowstorms to their anchorage in the wide Giudecca.

OUIDA, *SANTA BARBARA*, 1891

'THE MIRROR OF THE LAGOON . . .'

This strange, soft sea, so tempered into gentlehood, brings through its quietude another element of charm to Venice. It reflects all things with a wonderful perfection. Whatever loveliness is by its side it makes more lovely. Shallow itself, it seems deep; and the towers and palaces of Venice in all their colours descend and shine among other clouds and in another sky below. All outlines of sculpture and architecture, of embossment, in wall and window; all play of sunshine and shade; all the human life in balcony, bridge or quay, on barge or boat, are in the waters as in a silent dream – revealed in every line and colour, but with an exquisite difference in softness and purity. All Nature's doings in the sky are also repeated with a tender fidelity in the mirror of the Lagoon – morning light, noonday silver, purple thunder cloud in the afternoon, sunset vapours, the moon and stars of night – and not only on the surface, but also, it seems, in an immeasurable depth. To look over the side of the boat into the water is to cry, 'I see infinite space.'

STOPFORD AUGUSTUS BROOKE, *THE SEA CHARM OF VENICE*, 1907

MORNING MISTS

The winter climate of Venice is notorious. A harsh, raw, damp miasma overcomes the city for weeks at a time, only occasionally dispersed by days of cold sunny brilliance. The rain teems down with a particular wetness, like unto like, stirring the mud in the bottom of the Grand Canal, and streaming magnificently off the marbles of the Basilica. The fog marches in forwardly from the sea, so thick that you cannot see across the Piazza, and the *vaporetto* labours towards the Rialto with an anxious look-out in the bows. Sometimes a layer of snow covers the city, giving it a certain sense of improper whimsy, as if you were to dress a duchess in pink ruffles. Sometimes the fringe of a *bora* sweeps the water in fierce waves up the narrower canals, and throws the moored boats viciously against the quays. The nights are vaporous and tomb-like, and the days dawn monotonously grey.

JAMES MORRIS, *VENICE*, 1960

ETERNAL VENICE

In the still canals the gorgeous palaces continually gaze down upon their own reflected images with placid satisfaction, and look with calm indifference upon the changing generations of men and women that glide upon the waters. The mists gather upon the mysterious lagoons and sink away again before the devouring light, day after day, year after year, century after century; and Venice is always there herself, sleeping or waking, laughing, weeping, dreaming, singing or sighing, living her own life through ages, with an intensely vital personality which time has hardly modified, and is altogether powerless to destroy.

FRANCIS MARION CRAWFORD, *GLEANINGS FROM VENETIAN HISTORY*, 1905

The only way to care for Venice as she deserves it is to give her a chance to touch you often – to linger and remain and return.

HENRY JAMES, *ITALIAN HOURS*, 1882

ACKNOWLEDGEMENTS

PICTURE CREDITS

Front cover: *Gondolas on the Grand Canal*, Peder Monsted (Fine Art Photographic Library)
Back cover: *The Piazzetta and Doges' Palace*, James Holland (Bridgeman Art Library/Fine Art Society)
Frontispiece: *Venice*, H. B. Brabazon (Chris Beetles Ltd)
3: *Moored gondolas*, John Sims
5: *The Piazetta and Doges' Palace*, James Holland (Bridgeman/Fine Art Society)
7: *Figures near the Porta della Carta, Doges' Palace*, Walter Tyndale (Chris Beetles Ltd)
9: *The Horses of St Mark's*, Anon. (Fine Art Photographic)
11. *The Doges' Palace*, Michelangelo Durazzo (John Hillelson Agency)
13: *The North-west Porch of St Mark's*, John Ruskin (The Brantwood Trust, Coniston)
15: *Interior of St Mark's*, Albert Goodwin (Chris Beetles Ltd)
17: *Santa Maria della Salute*, John Yates (Susan Griggs Agency)
18: *Palace window*, John Sims
19: *The Palazzo Contarini*, Claude Monet (Kunstmuseum, St Gallen)
21: *The Grand Canal, near the Rialto*, Samuel Prout (Sotheby's)
23: *Umbrellas in the Rain (Ponte della Paglia)*, Maurice Brazil Prendergast (Museum of Fine Arts, Boston)
25: *The Basilica of St Mark's*, Fernand-Marie-Eugène Legout (Fine Art Photographic)
27: *Venetian backwaters*, John Sims
29: *Venice: The Bridge of Sighs*, J. M. W. Turner (Tate Gallery)
31: *Gondolas on the Grand Canal*, Peder Monsted (Fine Art Photographic)
33: *An Elegant Lady*, G. V. Pauli (Sotheby's)
34: *The Voga Lunga*, Michelangelo Durazzo (John Hillelson Agency)

35: *Festa della Regatta*, John Singer Sargent (Coe Kerr Gallery, New York)
37: *Venice: A Regatta on the Grand Canal*, Antonio Canaletto (National Gallery)
38: *The Carnival*, François Gailliard (Fine Art Photographic)
39: *The Carnival, Venice*, Georges Clairin (Sotheby's)
40: *Carnival mask*, Mark Cator (Impact Photos)
41: *Carnival fancy dress*, Horst Munzig (Susan Griggs Agency)
43: *Le Palais Blanc*, Henri Le Sidanier (Private Collection; Photo: Christie's Colour Library)
45: *Decay in Venice*, Adam Woolfitt (Susan Griggs Agency)
47: *The Canal Tolentini*, Franz Richard Unterberger (Bridgeman/Christie's)
49: *Venice on a Grey Day*, John Singer Sargent (Bridgeman/National Trust)
51: *Lagoon Scene*, Gugliemo Ciardi (Christie's)
53: *Misty morning in Venice*, Jake Rajs (Image Bank)
55: *Church of San Giorgio Maggiore, Venice*, Claude Monet (Bridgeman/National Gallery of Wales, Cardiff)

TEXT CREDITS

Text extracts from the following sources are reprinted with the kind permission of the publishers and copyright holders stated. Should any copyright holder have been inadvertently omitted they should apply to the publishers who will be pleased to credit them in full in any subsequent editions.

24: Mary McCarthy, *Venice Observed* (William Heinemann, 1961); 26, 42: Marcel Proust, *Remembrance of Things Past* (translated by Terence Kilmartin, © Chatto & Windus and Random House, Inc, 1981); 42: James Morris, *Venice* (Faber & Faber, 1960).

First U.S. Edition

Library of Congress Cataloguing-in-Publication Data is available.

ISBN 1-55970-010-6

Published in the United States by Arcade Publishing, Inc., New York,
a Little, Brown company.

10   9   8   7   6   5   4   3   2   1

Conceived, edited and designed by Russell Ash and Bernard Higton
Printed in Spain by Cayfosa, Barcelona